Reading Champion

Rumpelstiltskin and the Baby

by Damian Harvey and Tom Heard

W

FRANKLIN WATTS

LONDON•SYDNEY

Once upon a time there was a poor miller. His daughter was very good at spinning thread. The miller had a plan to get rich.

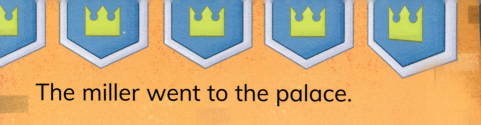

The miller went to the palace.

"My daughter is very clever. She can spin straw into gold!" he told the king.

"Bring her to the palace," said the king.

The king took the miller's daughter

to a room full of straw.

"Spin this straw into gold," he said.

Then the king locked the door and left.

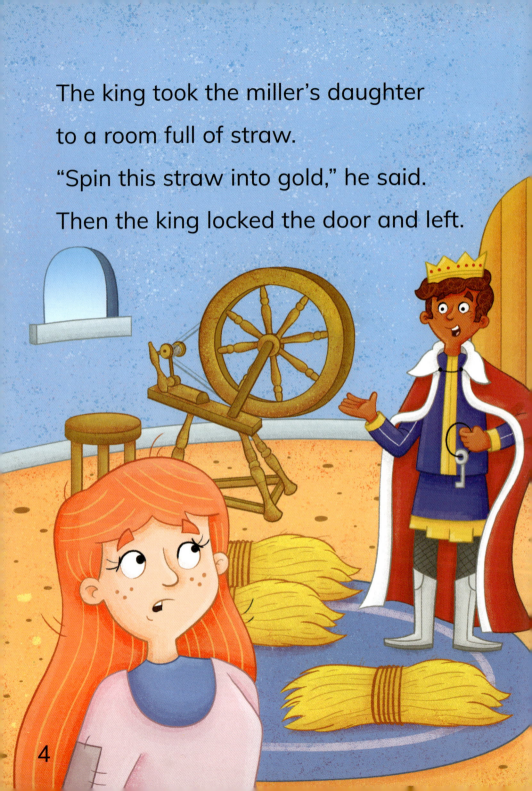

The miller's daughter sat down and cried.

"I can't spin straw into gold," she said.

"I will be locked in here forever."

Suddenly, there was a flash

and a strange little man appeared.

"Don't be sad," said the little man.
"I'll help you. But you must give me
something in return."
"I will give you my bracelet,"
said the miller's daughter.
"It is all that I have."

The little man smiled and put
the bracelet in his pocket.
Then he spun the straw into gold.

The king was very happy when he saw all the gold. But he was greedy and wanted more.

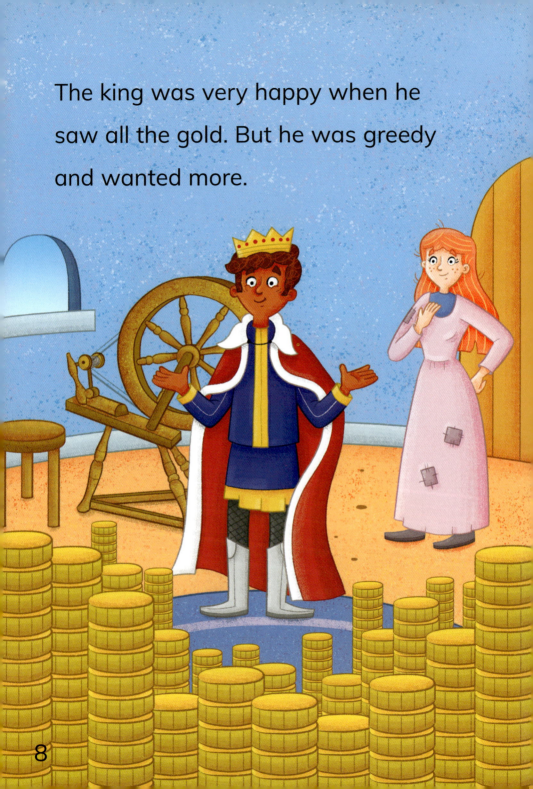

He took the miller's daughter to
a bigger room. It was full of straw.
"Now spin this straw into gold,"
said the king.
Then he locked the door and went away.

Suddenly, there was a flash, and
the strange little man appeared again.
"Don't be sad," said the little man.
"I will help you again."
But the miller's daughter started to cry.
"I have nothing left to give you,"
she said.

"When you have a baby," replied the man, "let me choose their name." The miller's daughter promised that she would.

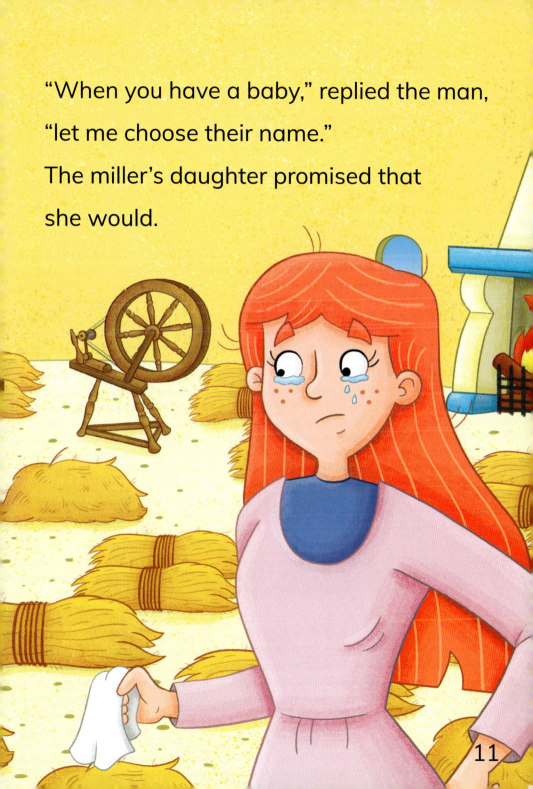

The king was very happy with the
miller's daughter. He fell in love with her.
Soon they were married.
The miller's daughter was happy.
She forgot about the strange little man.

Before long, the miller's daughter
had a little baby boy.
Then one day, as she rocked the baby
to sleep, the little man appeared again.
Then she remembered her promise.

"I have a name for your baby,"
said Rumpelstiltskin. "Stinkweed!"
"That's not a nice name,"
said the miller's daughter. She began to cry.
The little man felt sorry for her.
"If you can guess my name, you can
choose your baby's name," he said.
"I will come back tomorrow."

As the little man walked away from the palace, he sang a song.

"Rumpelstiltskin is my name,
and I am going to win this game."
He did not see that the miller's daughter had followed him.

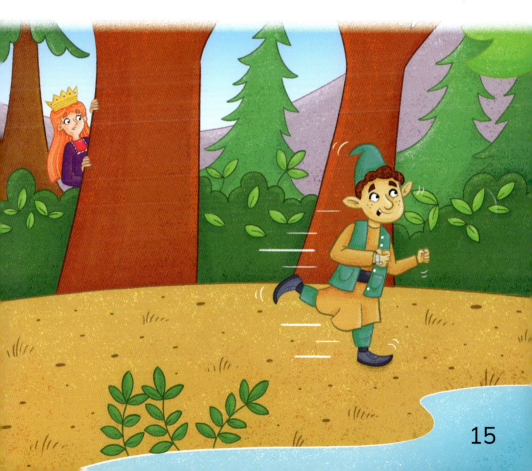

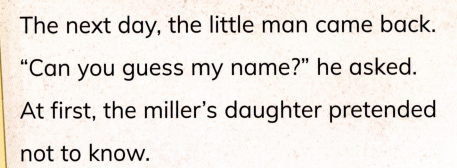

The next day, the little man came back.

"Can you guess my name?" he asked.

At first, the miller's daughter pretended not to know.

But then she said, "Is it Rumpelstiltskin?"

"Yes!" cried the little man. "Now you can choose a name for your baby."
"I think we will call him Finn," said the miller's daughter. Rumpelstiltskin smiled. "That is a much better name," he said.

"I have a gift for your baby,"
said Rumpelstiltskin.
He put his hand into his pocket and
took out the bracelet that
the miller's daughter had given him.

"That is perfect," said the miller's daughter.

"He will wear it every day. And you can

come and see him every day."

"Thank you," said Rumpelstiltskin.

"That would be perfect too."

Story order

Look at these 5 pictures and captions.
Put the pictures in the right order
to retell the story.

1

Rumpelstiltskin brings a gift for the baby.

2

The queen had forgotten about
her promise.

3

Rumpelstiltskin spins the straw into gold.

4

The queen hears Rumpelstiltskin's name.

5

Rumpelstiltskin wants to choose
the baby's name.

Independent Reading

This series is designed to provide an opportunity for your child to read on their own. These notes are written for you to help your child choose a book and to read it independently.

In school, your child's teacher will often be using reading books which have been banded to support the process of learning to read. Use the book band colour your child is reading in school to help you make a good choice. *Rumpelstiltskin and the Baby* is a good choice for children reading at Purple Band in their classroom to read independently. The aim of independent reading is to read this book with ease, so that your child enjoys the story and relates it to their own experiences.

About the book

When Rumpelstiltkin offers to help the miller's daughter spin straw into gold, she promises him something in return ... to let him name her first child. When Rumpelstiltkin returns to visit the baby, has he changed his mind?

Before reading

Help your child to learn how to make good choices by asking: "Why did you choose this book? Why do you think you will enjoy it?" Look at the cover together and ask: "What do you think the story will be about?" Ask your child to think of what they already know about the story context. Then ask your child to read the title aloud. Ask: "Why do you think the baby is important?" Remind your child that they can sound out the letters to make a word if they get stuck. Decide together whether your child will read the story independently or read it aloud to you.

During reading

Remind your child of what they know and what they can do independently. If reading aloud, support your child if they hesitate or ask for help by telling the word. If reading to themselves, remind your child that they can come and ask for your help if stuck.

After reading

Support comprehension by asking your child to tell you about the story. Use the story order puzzle to encourage your child to retell the story in the right sequence, in their own words. The correct sequence can be found on the next page. Give your child a chance to respond to the story: "What was your favourite part and why? What would have happened if Rumpelstitskin hadn't spun the straw into gold?" Help your child think about the messages in the book that go beyond the story and ask: "Why does Rumpelstiltskin change his mind about calling the baby 'Stinkweed'? What name would you give the baby? Why did you choose that name?"

Extending learning

Think about the story with your child, and make comparisons with *Rumpelstiltskin* if this story is known to them. Help your child understand the story structure by using the same story patterning and adding different elements. "Let's make up a new story about Rumpelstiltskin. Who might he help? What could he do? What would he get in return?" In the classroom, your child's teacher may be teaching different kinds of sentences. There are many examples in this book that you could look at with your child, including statements, commands and questions. Find these together and point out how the end punctuation can help us decide what kind of sentence it is.

Franklin Watts
First published in Great Britain in 2024
Hodder and Stoughton

Series Editors: Jackie Hamley and Melanie Palmer
Development Editors and Series Advisors: Dr Sue Bodman and Glen Franklin
Series Designers: Cathryn Gilbert and Peter Scoulding

A CIP catalogue record for this book is
available from the British Library.

ISBN 978 1 4451 9091 4 (hbk)
ISBN 978 1 4451 9093 8 (pbk)
ISBN 978 1 4451 9092 1 (ebook)

Printed in China

Franklin Watts
An imprint of
Hachette Children's Group
Part of Hodder and Stoughton
Carmelite House
50 Victoria Embankment
London EC4Y 0DZ

An Hachette UK Company
www.hachette.co.uk

www.reading-champion.co.uk

FSC
www.fsc.org
MIX
Paper | Supporting
responsible forestry
FSC® C104740

Answer to story order: 3,5,2,4,1